Text copywrite 2016 by Sara Ison and Dianna Rosenbaum
Illustrations copywrite by Rachel Alford
All rights reserved published by RoseIson
ISBN-13: 978-0692806661 (RoseIson)
ISBN-10: 0692806660

All rights reserved. No part of this book may be reproduced in any form or by any electronic or mechanical means, including information storage and retrieval systems, without permission in writing from the publisher, except by reviewers, who may quote brief passages in a review.

This book is based on a true story and is dedicated in loving memory to a wonderful, loving and caring woman who taught us right from wrong, who was there for us all through both the good and the bad times. The person who is responsible for this story, who is known as Mother and Mamawl, Pauletta Schuyler. We miss and love you dearly and hope you too have lots of feathers on your angel wings.

In a small town called Tallahassee, there was an eight-year-old beautiful dark haired little girl named Ashley. Ashley went to daycare with her brother Lee in the morning because her mother and Mamawl had to go to work and then she would go to school from the daycare.

She wanted to have lots of friends so she told the other children at daycare that her family was famous and rich and she could get them whatever they wanted. She said "If you will be my friend I will get you all the candy and toys you want". All the kids promised to be her friend and Ashley loved all the attention she was getting from the other children who wanted to be her friend just because she promised to get them the things they wanted.

Ashley started stealing from stores, from her Mamawl, Mother and her brother so she could give the candy and toys to her friends. She would show off everything she had stolen just to make her friends believe that her family really was famous and rich and she could get everything and anything she wanted.

The children wanted her to bring them toys and candy all the time. They told Ashley if she didn't bring them things they wouldn't be her friend anymore. So Ashley started stealing and lying even more to bring them what they wanted and she started making up bigger stories and lies than she did before to get even more friends.

One day Ashley started feeling bad about what she was doing and she could not keep up with the demands of her friends. Ashley started to feel really scared that her friends would find out the truth about her and she would not have any friends left. She ran to her Mamawl and told her Mamawl all the stories she had told and all the stealing she had done and that she was sorry she had done these things. She explained to her Mamawl that she just wanted to have lots of friends and she thought if she got the things the other children wanted, they would all be her friends. Ashley's Mamawl thought about this all night.

The next morning Ashley, her brother Lee, Mother and Mamawl got in the car to go to Daycare. Ashley's Mamawl said "I have thought a lot about what you told me yesterday and though I am disappointed that you have lied, told stories and stolen, I still love you very much and I would like to tell you a story and I want you to listen. When you go to Heaven you will get your Angel Wings. God keeps your angel wings with him and when you steal, lie and do selfish things God takes feathers from your wings and when you tell the truth, do the right things and do good deeds for others, God adds feathers to your wings. The more you do the right things and tell the truth the more feathers God will add to your angel wings".

"But what if my friends don't like me anymore when I tell them the truth?" asked Ashley.

"Then they really were not your true friends and you do not need friends who want you just because you give them things" replied Mamawl.

Ashley began to think really hard about her angel wings. She wondered if she had any feathers on her wings and how she would fly around Heaven if she had no feathers on her angel wings. She didn't want to have scruffy, featherless wings, she wanted her wings to be fluffy and beautiful and full of feathers so she would be able to fly everywhere in Heaven. They finally arrived at the daycare and as they were getting out of the car, Ashley looked up and saw a single beautiful pure white, small fluffy feather floating down from the sky.

"Look" she yelled and they all saw a single feather floating down slowly and they watched in amazement as the feather lightly touched the hood of her Mamawl's car and then shot straight back up into heaven very fast. They watched the feather going straight up until they could no longer see it. There was no breeze or wind to carry the feather up, there was no bird in the trees above the car which the feather could have come from. They looked at each other in puzzlement because they could not figure out where the white feather came from or how it came down and went straight up, but in their hearts they knew the feather was a sign from God to Ashley that he did indeed keep her angel wings with him.

Ashley knew for sure right then that she needed to start doing what was right and telling the truth. As Ashley walked into daycare that morning, all her friends were excited to see her and waiting for their candy and toys that Ashley had promised them.

Ashley told her friends how sorry she was that she had lied to them. "My family is not famous or rich and I just wanted to have some friends" she said. "I know I may not have any friends now but I'm not going to steal or tell anymore lies". Some of her friends mumbled and groaned and walked away from her. Some of them were mean, called her names and told her that they would no longer be her friends, but some of them stayed with her and told her that it was alright and they would still like to be her friends.

Though she lost a few of her friends that day she gained some new and true friends that stayed her friends because they liked her for who she was and not for what she could or could not give them.

Ashley learned a lot that day and she felt much better because she now knew that she did not have to lie and steal to fit in with her friends. She learned that making friends isn't by buying their friendship with candy and toys and true friends like you just for who you are. She learned that sometimes people just wanted to be her friend for what she could give them and those are not real friends.

Before she told a lie or stole she would stop herself and think about God's feathers and her angel wings that are waiting for her in Heaven. From then on Ashley told the truth, she did not tell anymore stories and didn't steal because she wants her angel wings to have lots of feathers when she goes to Heaven to put them on.

No matter what you do or what you say, God is always there with you. When you feel that tingle in your head and in your heart, that is God's way of telling you that what you are about to do or have done is wrong and you need to either not do that or you will need to make it right by telling the truth and God will always be there to help guide you. Sometimes God will send little messages to let you know that he is around for you. God loves you very much and will always forgive you.

www.ingramcontent.com/pod-product-compliance
Lightning Source LLC
Chambersburg PA
CBHW041233040426
42444CB00002B/143